LETTERS TO THE PRESIDENT ABOUT ABORTION

By Dale E. Watson

ISBN 978-1-62806-159-8

Cover image of White House: public domain image via Wikipedia user

Author Contact Information:
Dale E. Watson
PO Box 926
Salisbury, MD 21803-0926
Phone: (410) 546-4694
Fax: (410) 749-5737
Email: dalewatson@verizon.net

TABLE OF CONTENTS

Introduction
- 7 -

Letter to the President dated June 29, 2017
- 8 -

Letter to the President dated October 18, 2017
- 11 -

Urgent Action Needed by the Body of Christ
- 18 -

The Cure
- 22 -

Conclusion
- 24 -

Jesus's Involvement with Men,
Women, and Nations
- 26 -

Prayer
- 29 -

INTRODUCTION

I have written this in an attempt to stir the body of Christ to further understand what the ravages of abortion is doing to the United States.

I have kept this book brief and a quick study to that end.

Remember, Jesus is in control. The body of Christ only has to call on him.

All Bible quotes are from the King James Version.

June 29, 2017

President Donald J. Trump
White House
1600 Pennsylvania Ave
Washington, D.C. 20500

Dear President Trump;

I would like to congratulate you for your victory to the Presidency. Also I would like to congratulate you on your performance and your numerous victories.

I am writing to thank you for your pro-life stance. You are the only President since Roe vs. Wade to take a strong stand on the life issue.

You see I believe that the Lord Jesus has already brought blessings to the U.S.A. as a result of your position and will continue to do so.

I am talking about the rains that the Lord has sent. You see the Lord Jesus controls the weather. Within a couple of months after your inauguration, California has declared the State drought free. Within a few days, California reservoirs were overflowing.

The Washington Post article dated 4/16/2017

stated "more than sixty (60) feet of snow has piled up on the peaks of the Sierra Nevada since October."

"Across the Northern Sierra Region – an average of eight different climate stations – 87.9 inches of rain fell, making this winter the wettest on record"

The Washington Post article dated 4/8/2017 states "Governor Jerry Brown declared an end to the California drought Friday, lifting emergency orders that had forced residents to stop running sprinklers as often and encouraged them to rip out thirsty lawns during the States driest period on record."

I saw a quote somewhere that they would be snow skiing in California until July.

In addition to the rain, the melting snow would replenish the streams flowing down the mountains which would keep the water supply up.

Wild flowers gave beautiful color to the mountains.

The rest of the countries benefited as well. An article in *USA Today – The Daily Times* an article states on 4/28/2017 "Drought in the U.S. fell to a record low this week. Just 6.1 % of the 48 contiguous states is currently experiencing such dry conditions federal officials said Thursday."

The same article goes on to state "The current record low is in sharp contrast to September 2012 when drought reached a record high – 65.5% - in the U.S."

President Trump – water is the main substance of life. We consume it. Crops and animals need it. I know you are busy, but take a few minutes and listen to the brooks trickling down the mountain; or the water going over a dam; or the beating of the Ocean Waves on the shore.

The same Jesus Christ that created the earth and the universe is the same one who previously flooded the whole earth, parted the red sea so the ancient Israelites could cross on dry ground and calmed the seas and wind when he was in the boat with his disciples.

I believe this year, we will have a bumper crop. The Lord will truly bless this Nation.

I would suggest you give pro-life speeches whenever you can.

Thank you for being pro-life!

God Bless,
Dale E. Watson

October 18, 2017

President Donald J. Trump
White House
1600 Pennsylvania Ave
Washington, D.C. 20500

Dear President Trump;

I wrote you previously thanking you for being the first pro-life president.

I am writing you this time to inform you regarding the ravages of abortions on U.S. Society.

I direct you to the first murder, Cain killed his brother Abel. Chapter 4, vs 8-12 records the following:

> v8. And Cain talked with Abel his brother: and it came to pass when they were in the field that Cain rose up against Abel his brother, and slew him.
>
> v9. And the Lord said unto Cain, where is Abel thy brother? And he said, I know not: Am I my brother's

keeper?

v10. And he said, what hast thou done? The voice of thy brother's blood crieth unto me from the ground.

v11. And now art thou cursed from the earth, which hath opened her mouth to receive thy brother's blood from thy hand;

v12. When thou tillest the ground it shall not henceforth yield unto thee her strength......

Since Roe vs. Wade was decided in January 1973 there have been approximately sixty million (60,000,000) abortions. Can you imagine the blood of all those individuals crying to the Lord. Just take a few minutes and contemplate this.

For punishment the Lord told him "when thou tillest the ground, it shall not henceforth yield unto thee her strength...

This was the first inflation. In other words, he would put the same inputs and effort into the ground and it would yield less. For example, instead of one hundred (100) bushels per acre, he would only get seventy five (75).

Can we pin point major inflation in the US after January, 1973:

In an article entitled "The Great Inflation of

the 1970's" written by Gregory Bresiger, he states that the inflation started December 1972/January 1973. Quoting Gregory Bresinger "in 1973 inflation more than doubled to 8.8%. Later in the decade it would go to 12%. By 1980 inflation was 14%. Interest rates shot up to 20% foreclosing a lot of people out of new cars and homes."

In 1973 there was a gasoline shortage. There were gas lines at gas stations. The stations would run out of gas. There were odd days and even days. 10 years prior to 1973 the price of a gallon of gas remained fairly stable at $.34 - $.36 per gallon. In 1973 it rose to $.39, 1974 $.53 and 1981 it was $1.31.

The average price of a house in 1973 was $29,900.00. By 1981 it was $67,600.00.

The average price of a car in 1973 was $4052.00. In 1981 the average price was $8910.00.

To buy a car or house interest rates were close to 20%.

The above costs were not supply and demand driven.

The average wage in 1973 was $7,580.16. The average wage in 1981 was $13,773.10. This is an increase of $6,192.97.

Mr. President I am sure you remember President Nixon encouraging people to turn down the thermostat and putting an extra sweater on. He also lowered speed limits to 55MPH. Also President Ford passed out WIN buttons (Whip Inflation Now).

Abortions spiked in the 1970's.

The Bible teaches that the Lord hates the shedding of innocent blood.

Some effects of the shedding of blood in the Bible are: King David was deprived of the privilege of building the original Jewish temple (I chronicle ch.22, v.8) "But the word of the Lord came to me, (King David), saying thou hast shed blood abundantly and hast made great wars. Thou shall not build a house unto my name, because they hast shed much blood upon the earth in my sight". In II Kings, ch 21, v16 "moreover Manesseh shed innocent blood very much, till he had filled Jerusalem from one end to another...."And in II Kings ch. 24, v4"And also for the innocent blood that he (Manesseh) shed: for he filled Jerusalem with innocent blood: which the Lord would not pardon."

Since Roe vs. Wade (January 1973) there has been approximately 60,000,000 abortions. In January 2018 it will be 45 years of virtually unlimited abortion. More than half of those souls would be of child bearing years. If half (ie: 30,000,000) had one child each then the U.S. is minus an additional 30,000,000 souls. There could be as many as 10,000,000 grandchildren. To make it Simple:

$$
\begin{array}{r}
60,000,000 \\
30,000,000 \\
\underline{10,000,000} \\
100,000,000
\end{array}
$$

The above is not scientific, but you get the point. The U.S. population is down approximately 25% because of abortion. The population of the U.S. currently is 325,000,000. It should be approximately 430,000,000. There is approximately 1,000,000 abortions per year. Catholic News Channel reported on 6/11/2017 that there had been as many abortions to date as all of 2016. Are we headed to two million abortions for 2017.

Other affects are for the last 5 years there are more deaths than births in the white and black communities. There are about as many millennials as boomers. So when all the boomers are drawing social security, there could be a tax revolt with the millennials.

I believe that if a statistician computed the numbers, that in 20 years the population could be down 35-40%.

Economically the U.S. would collapse.

The U.S. has had a holocaust of the shedding of innocent blood (60,000,000 plus souls).

The Bible also teaches that individuals and nations reap what they sow. Also it says if you sow the wind you reap the whirl wind. It is no wonder that we have so much violence in the streets on the U.S. Also from a economic point of view our economy is at a tipping point of collapsing.

Mr. President, I implore you to stop abortion with an executive order. This would right to economy and stop the violence in the streets. By the time that it would reach the Supreme Court, I believe that it would be upheld.

Jeremiah Ch.1 vs.4&5 states:

> vs 4 "Then the word of the Lord came unto me, saying,"
> vs 5 "Before I formed thee in the belly I knew thee; and before thou camest forth out of the womb I sanctified thee, and I ordained thee a prophet unto nations."

Jesus Christ creates our soul and then places it in our physical body's when he creates our body in our mother's womb. Abortion destroys the Lord's creation. I wonder how many prophets were destroyed from abortion.

I have been in constant prayer for you and your protection and that the Lord would give you the wisdom to right our country. I believe the elimination of abortion would be a major start.

Thank you for your time.

Yours truly,
Dale E. Watson

P.S. Please reread the above and contemplate on the numbers.

Urgent Action Needed
By The Body of Christ

If someone punched a pregnant woman in the stomach and her baby died as a result, the individual would be charged, convicted, and sent to prison (or executed) for First Degree Murder. Something appears to be wrong with this picture. A pregnant woman has a right to do the same thing without punishment. An abortion doctor and staff can perform the same thing. The U.S. Treasury is being used for the same thing as well as many State Treasuries. Pharmacies sell the "day after pill" for women to take for the same result up to certain number of days after having unprotected sex.

If you Google the population of the United States for the following years, then you get:

1970 - 203,392,031
1980 - 226,545,805
1990 - 248,709,873
2000 - 281,421,906
2010 - 308,745,539
2017 - 325,000,000 (est)

From 1970 to the present the United States population has increased 122,000,000 (est).

If there had been no abortion the U.S. population should have approximately doubled the 122,000,000 to an increase of 244,000,000.

Projecting into the future twenty (20) years the population loss to the U.S. population would look like the following:

At the current rate of abortion at 1,000,000 per year, in 20 years there would be another loss of live births of 20,000,000. The total number of abortions since Roe vs. Wade would be 80,000,000. This would be sixty five (65) years since Roe vs Wade. Using age twenty (20) and above as being child bearing age, 55,000,000 could have had one child. This would add another fifty five (55) million to the total population loss. Forty (40) years from sixty five (65) years equals twenty five (25). There could be twenty five (25) million grandchildren. Subtracting twenty (20) from twenty five (25) equals five (5) years. There would then be a minimum of five (5) million great grandchildren. The following is what the total numbers would look like:

Abortions - 80,000,000
Children - 55,000,000
G.Children - 25,000,000
Great G Children - 5,000,000

Total Population Reduction - 165,000,000 (est)

The above is not scientific, but you get the picture. Frankly, I believe that the numbers are much higher. We have no idea how to track the actual number of abortions.

Young lady or woman, if you have been deceived into having an abortion you have murdered your baby. Jesus created that baby. Jesus can forgive you for having the abortion. Where you are sitting just bow your head and say, "Jesus I have sinned against you. Please forgive me for my sins and sin of abortion. And come into my life and be Lord of my Life. In Jesus precious name, Amen."

A tremendous load will be lifted from you.

President Trump is a pro-life President. He is actively promoting the pro-life agenda. He wants to economically improve the life of U.S. citizens. I believe that things are improving. However the wages in the U.S. are flatlined. That means wages are just keeping up with inflation. The Federal Reserve has been raising interest because they believe that inflation is going to rise. This will cause wages to fall behind.

What can we do to improve the economy? The first thing is to outlaw all abortions. The Lord will bless the U.S. Also, we will have younger workers to grow the economy, otherwise we will end up on the trash heap of history.

Psalms chapter 33, V.12: "Blessed is the nation whose God is the Lord."

One of the Ten Commandments is "Thou shall not kill."

But... "Murders" shall have their part in the lake which burneth with fire and brimstone: (hell) Revelation ch 21 V. 8.

THE CURE

In order to cure the economic problems in the United States, I am calling on the body of Christ to fast and pray for thirty (30) days from March 1 through March 30, 2018. Fasting and praying doesn't have to mean stop eating although this is one way. It only means doing something sacrificial. It could mean giving up only certain foods such as desserts or not eating out for the thirty (30) days. It could mean giving up your favorite TV show or the movies. Remember Jesus said, "Don't fast and pray like the Pharisees with a big show." Rather fast and pray quietly and going about your daily routine as normal.

While you fast, I would request that you quietly pray three (3) times per day (i.e. morning, noon and night).

- Suggested Prayer -

Dear Father,

Stop all abortions in the United States. Remove all people of authority from government (such as judges, whether Supreme Court, Federal Court of Appeals, District Court, and State Court judges that support abortion) and all legislatures such as U.S. Congress, U.S. Senate,

State Legislatures and any Municipal Legislative bodies, individuals who support abortion. In addition remove all individuals in this Country who support abortion.

In Jesus name I pray.

Amen

Unless the above individuals repent of their sins and ask Jesus into their lives to be Lord of their life, they should be removed. How they are removed is up to Jesus.

As Christians, we need to pray for these individuals, lift them up to the Lord and turn them over to him. Revenge is mine sayeth the Lord.

During the above thirty (30) days, I am requesting that all churches remain open twenty four (24) hours per day to receive those that desire to repent and have a brief period of consultation. Also churches are encouraged to have revivals during the above-mentioned period.

Conclusion

I AM SURE MOST OF US LOVE America and that we want a strong economy and we want the violence in the streets to stop. Stopping abortion will correct many of these problems. People who enforce and support abortion are guilty of murder in the eyes of the Lord Jesus Christ. Remember he is in control. We only have to ask him. He can move mountains (abortion).

I am asking the whole body of Christ whether in the United States or around the world to join in this fast. If you read this book after March 30, 2018, please fast and pray.

The survival of the United States depends on it. It has been forty five (45) years since Roe vs. Wade. Forty (40) years is a biblical number such as the Israelites wandering in the desert for refusal to take the promised land. I believe that we are at a tipping point. Remember Jesus is in control.

An article in *The Washington Post* on December 29, 2017 entitled "Lots of work but not enough workers," describes a number of industries with openings going unfilled because of no workers. The cause is abortion.

Several guests on business channels indicate that U.S. birth rate is not high enough to carry out President Trump's economic agenda.

Remember it is Jesus's desire that none should perish.

Right now, kneel where you are and recite the sinner's prayers:

"Lord Jesus, I confess that I am a sinner.
Forgive me my sins (especially abortion),
come into my life and be Lord of my life.
In Jesus name I pray,
Amen."

When conception occurs, a small bright light flashes and it looks like a cross.

How Jesus judges the participants in abortion and those supporting abortion is in his hands.

JESUS INVOLVEMENT WITH MEN, WOMAN, AND NATIONS

Jesus has always been involved with his creation as follows:

1. Jesus spoke and the Universe was created, including earth, man, and beast.

2. Jesus spoke and the flood came destroying all humanity, but eight (8) people on earth for man's evil ways.

3. Jesus spoke and the death angel moved over Egypt killing all the first born.

4. Jesus spoke and the Red Sea parted allowing the Israelis to cross to safety on dry ground.

5. Jesus spoke and the Jordan River ceased to flow to allow the Israelis to cross into the Promised Land on dry ground.

6. Jesus spoke and Mary become pregnant by the Holy Ghost.

7. Jesus spoke and the storm on the Galilee ceased, moving his Disciples to declare what manner of man is this that even the seas and winds obey him.

8. Jesus spoke and he arose from the grave.

9. Jesus spoke and The State of Israel came into existence on May 14,1948.

10. Jesus spoke and hyper-inflation occurred in the U.S. after the Supreme Court decided Roe vs. Wade in January 1973.

11. Jesus spoke and a storm suddenly appeared and destroyed the Bush summer home in Maine in October 1991.

12. Jesus spoke and hurricane Isabela came up the Chesapeake Bay in 2003. The eye went over Washington DC, driving President George W. Bush to Camp David. The Quartet led by President George W. Bush had been negotiating a Palestinian State in the Promised Land.

13. Jesus spoke and Hurricanes Katrina, Rita and Wilma slammed into the United States in 2005. President George W. Bush and the quartet had just pressured Prime Minister Ariel Sharon of Israel to forcefully remove all Jews out of the Gaza strip. Shortly thereafter, Ariel Sharon had a stroke from which he never recovered.

14. Jesus spoke and sent Hurricane Sandy up the East Coast of the United States and slammed into New Jersey and New York City.

When President Obama went there and met with the Governor of New Jersey, it raised his approval rating. This gave him the re-election to Presidency in 2012.

15. Jesus spoke and raised up the votes to put Donald Trump into the Presidency of the United States.

16. Let's pray and fast from March 1, 2018 through March 30, 2018 asking Jesus to speak and rid the United States of the scourge of abortion.

The above are just a few of the many examples that I could have cited. Jesus is in control.

PRAYER

We all confess that we are sinners.

Hear our prayer, O Lord.

We thank you Jesus for coming to earth for our salvation.

Hear our prayer, O Lord.

Forgive us our sins of commission and omission and particular with regard to abortion.

Hear our prayer, O Lord.

We thank you Lord for forgiving us of our sins.

Hear our prayer, O Lord.

We give you all the praise, honor and glory for doing so.

Hear our prayer, O Lord.

www.ingramcontent.com/pod-product-compliance
Lightning Source LLC
Chambersburg PA
CBHW071449040426
42445CB00012BA/1499